THE
LIGHT
TEARS
LOOSE

Books by KB Ballentine

Almost Everything, Almost Nothing (2017), Middle Creek
Publishing
The Perfume of Leaving (2016), Blue Light Press
What Comes of Waiting (2013), Blue Light Press
Fragments of Light (2009), Celtic Cat Publishing
Gathering Stones (2008), Celtic Cat Publishing

Anthologies containing her work:

In Plein Air (2017)
Carrying the Branch: Poets in Search of Peace (2017)
In God's Hands (2017)
River of Earth and Sky: Poems for the Twenty-First Century
(2015)
Southern Poetry Anthology, Volume VI: Tennessee (2013)
Southern Light: Twelve Contemporary Southern Poets (2011)
A Tapestry of Voices (2011)

THE LIGHT TEARS LOOSE

KB BALLENTINE

Blue Light Press ⊕ 1st World Publishing

1st WORLD
PUBLISHING

San Rafael | Fairfield | Delhi

Winner of the 2016 Blue Light Press Book Award

1st World Library
PO Box 2211
Fairfield, Iowa 52556
www.1stworldpublishing.com

Blue Light Press
PO Box 150300
San Rafael, California 94915
bluelightpress.com

Cover and Page Design, Author Photo
Jim Canestrari

ISBN: 978-1-4218-3632-4

Library of Congress Control Number: 2019944602

For family and friends who have been part of the Light

Publication Acknowledgements

The author would like to thank the editors of the following publications in which some of these poems were previously published, sometimes in different forms:

"Between Us, the Moon" *Millwork*
"Blackberry Smoke," "My Lost Child" *Allegro*
"Blossoms, Laced with Snow," "Until the Raven Comes" *Jellyfish Whispers*
"Breathing the Dark" *Vitaminzzz*
"Brimming Dark" *Spank the Carp*
"Darkness, Roaming" *Inlandia*
"Darkness to Hold" *PoetryMagazine.com* Vol XXI
"Edge of Morning," "Green, Springing," "Shrine," "Where I Find Belief" *Avocet*
"Edged with Fire," "Faithful, Even As It Fades" *Poetry South*
"Fall Comes Weeping" *Heartland Review*
"Last Swallow of Light" *Outrider MOON Anthology*
"Let the Rain Possess Me," "The Light Tears Loose," "Remember the Stars" *Amethyst Review*
"Light Has No Mercy" *Tinderbox Poetry Journal*
"Message to the Writer" *2nd and Church*
"My Hands, Cracked Cups" *Blue Heron Review*
"A Place to Breathe" *Razor Literary Magazine*
"Pointillism: Morning" *Nebo*
"Raiding the Dark" AFIELD
"Re-Creation" *Raconteur Magazine*
"Something Possible" *Parentheses Journal*
"Spring, Slouching" *Gyroscope Review*
"Storing the Dark" *Inscape Magazine*
"Summer Pours Out" *3Elements*
"Time is a Crooked Thing" *Linnet's Wings*
"The Uncertain Hour" *Bloodroot Lit Journal*
"The Weight of Snow" *Heartland Review*

The skies are painted with unnumber'd sparks.

William Shakespeare, *Julius Caesar* III, i, 68

Contents

III. DARKER

IV. MORE LIGHT

Everything Possible

Fireflies belong to the night,
but morning wastes no time as wrens sing
awake the fields, the woods.
Sparrows thorn the sky —
silhouettes etched into the blue.
And our sphere widens …

I. LIGHT

The Light Tears Loose

Every now and then / I see a sunset / and I want to crawl inside of myself / and match that kind of glowing. —James Diaz

Evening sun divides the horizon,
shadows whispering the lawn,
that last blaze burning the sky.

The air sparks —
the cosmos no longer contains me,
and my soul twists in longing …

A bend in the road surprises with fields of poppies —
awe swelling when I breathe wren-song,
listen to violets unfolding.

And when the light finally flares, then disappears,
I am the craggy mountain, the grain of sand
lapped into the ocean. An ember
arcing, illuminating the deep.

Holding the Tide of Night

Moonshadows shift the yard, the field,
the wood beyond. Grackles flutter and fuss
somewhere close. Two deer
etch the horizon, deeper silhouettes.
Give me your hand.

At lake's edge, frogs hum and chant, then pause
their song as we stir the air.
Fingers and lips explore, caress.
Clothes abandoned
one by one until desire
                        explodes.

We slip, hand in hand, into the cool water,
and the frogs revive their chorus.
An owl echoes the wind.
Around us, night collapses, stars crowding closer —
Dizzy with their glare, we gasp,
grasp at these scraps of promise.
Hear the sky sigh our names.

The Memory of Scent

First thing on a blueberry morning,
fog silences the crescent moon,
dew poised like pearls, like chips of diamonds
in the half-light.
Something scurries in the shadows — raccoon or possum —
blinded by porch lights, sidewalks steaming.
Stones softened with moss, with fern,
lilacs and promise trace the dawn.

Something Possible

The cost of love is the sea kissing
the shore, a little bit left, a little more
taken away. Here and gone, whispers
of foam and spray.

Each morning, windows open to the ocean,
I gaze at a horizon that merges water and sky
into one thin stitch — indistinct, indefinable.
In the evening the surf confesses
in ebb and flow its take-all-or-leave-it promises.

I am ensnared by this murmur, this roar,
this peak and trough. This restlessness.
This constancy. This ever-present pulsing
desire.

Morning Burning

Air wrinkles in June's dawn,
horizon fringed a fire-engine red
swallowed by a flood of gold.
Crows jabber me awake,
tempt me into day-dew
where spider-silk pearls the hedgerows.
Hidden in hydrangeas, bees circle
shaded puddles, sip blossom-hearts.

Before the mowers and mulchers rumble,
before the grass dries, I enter
the wren's psalm, the squirrel's chuckle —
flashes of sound and stillness
coalescing then spiraling to the sky.

Blackberry Smoke

Blackberries plump the hedges,
      beeches curving across the trail.
A dried milkweed pod caught
      in the underbrush shifts shape,
mist closing in.
      I heard your voice yesterday so clearly,
I turned around.

      Dusk hushes the hills,
thrush hiding in the hedgerows
      swallowing her song.
Doves applaud the air.
      Nights like this — coffee filmed with chill
while you strummed the guitar, hummed
      as the moon echoed its light
            into mounting shadows.

Edged with Fire

Because maples have burst into flame,
     morning flushes long before the moon
   slides from her wide perch,
       stars stippling the bluing sky.

     Towhees sheltered in the Rose of Sharon
   tempt the sun with song,
     and wrens blend with fallen leaves
drifting into edges of the yard.

     Too early for frost, steam lingers
   over the birdbath where a squirrel sips,
    tail flirting the air, starlings
   stenciled on oak branches.

     Chrysanthemums crisp the lawn,
echo dawn's gold, Venus murmuring
                    goodbye.

Where I Find Belief —

in the rain as it spools late afternoons,
skies gray, blankets layered around me on the porch

in the bluebird as he hops in the water and wriggles
his feathers dry

in the silence of dawn's snowfall, everything wrapped
in lavender reflection, my nose pink and cold
while the trees   breathe

in puppies as they swarm and wiggle and lick —
puppy breath teasing my cheeks

in the honey-glow of evening's sunset,
shadows of pine lengthening, a barred owl calling,
calling in the night

Veil of Sleep

Rain peppers the roof, pocks my thoughts
with shadow, with loss. Before the fire
I warm my feet, gaze across the greening lawn.
Spring again, soon.

Hickory branches etch skeleton silhouettes
in gray skies, leaves still a coppery carpet
to shuffle on days that beckon us with fingers of sun.
Not today.

Today beads of water cling
to the windows, transparent tracks
chasing across the pane.
Deck lacquered with ice, I dare not
breach the bounds of these walls.
You there,
                    I here —

but we nod to each other in dreams.
An aura of hope envelopes sleep — you smiling,
arms open. I will meet you tonight.

Raiding the Dark

Hunger Moon hides behind the mountain —
golden haze haloing its silhouette.
We stumble to the car, grass stiff and brittle.
This afternoon will be 68, but right now
it's 23 degrees and the wind knifes right through
our coats, the newspaper's rage still rolled
in plastic.   There's a black hole somewhere
sucking in the light — stars and planets,
space dust disappearing faster than synapses collapse.
But here dawn sings in a wren's clear notes,
neighbor's porch light beckoning, fiery and bright.

Let the Rain Possess Me

Stars fading, a margin of sky clears
as clouds spill from the west.
Miles of blue for a week, warmest winter
on record, but now darkness swells,
shares a remnant of moon with gray dawn.

Black caps tapping at the feeder, chickadees
feint with goldfinches for the best fruit, seed.
The bluebirds never left, January so much
like early April. They just fluff and rustle
in the water, chatter to squirrels who burst
the length of hickory branches, leaves dried
and crackling but still hanging on.

Hanging on to joy, even with storms
moving in. They scrabble and loop the bark —
and the chase is on as drops scatter the yard
then more until silver hazes,   erases me.

My Lost Child

dances on the salt marsh,
peers between cord grass as she hides
and seeks between the dunes.
She hops with oyster catchers in foaming wavelets
and scurries across the sand with fiddler crabs.
She skips from the water over the wrack
to brush sea oats as they curve
and sway back in the wind.

Farther into the tree line, she dodges
saw palmettos, white pines until she discovers
the live oak, the stippled shade that veils
her freckles, her sun-bleached hair.
Silent as the deer she follows, she tilts her head
at the cicadas' garbled oaths, the sizzle
of waves rushing the shore.
Where she strokes the bark, moss appears —
then she is gone.

Whitecaps Cresting

Pelicans cough across the surf,
spray escaping in tendrils of salt
that clings to rocks, roots in crevices
until an almost-snow coats the cliffs.
A jogger puffs past, shoe prints
barely there then glazed and gone by rising tides.

The horizon hazes with late rain,
promise of a cooler evening.
Seaweed whiskers the shoreline,
sand pipers hopping in and out of the waves,
notes of the deep discovering
a bit of light in these last days.

Darkness to Hold

Listen to the stars breathing in the night.
Curse the dawn that steals your dreams
while rose and lavender unstitch
horizon's seam and bluebirds bunch
the feeder, one red-bellied woodpecker
tapping you awake.

You stumble into this world,
this life, this day. Trade vivid
visions for monochrome moments —
bliss orphaned, forgetfulness splintered.
The unblinking sun yawns.
Work calls you into eight by eight cubes:
time measured in ticks of two blades
dragging across a face, your skin, your thoughts.

Listen, listen to the stars, breathing
on the other side of the sky,
waiting with your dreams.
Nightingale and lark singing,
shadows knitting the dark.

Last Swallow of Light

We just wanted to be alone in that great shining emptiness.
—Arthur C Clark

Pinpricks of grace frame the Calming Moon.
Woods smolder with melodies of crickets
rimmed by a bass line of frogs, a fox's whine.
The breeze tousles thick leaves,
branches slanting like reeds at the shore.
Forget-me-nots and honesty bruise the moss
where ferns nestle, an exercise in stillness, patience.
One day I, too, will turn to the heavens,
let moonlight silver my face,
let the emptiness finally fill the rest of me —
I will be a wick, lit with an inner blaze
until all that's left is smoke and ash.

18   The Light Tears Loose

II. DARK

Faithful, Even As It Fades

Last splendor of leaves spool like gypsy moths
from mountain ash, from oak sparking gold-orange-red.
October now, even Virginia creeper folds into shadows
that sever the edges of our yard, fields furrowed
and empty after the harvest. You are closer somehow
under this bright blue sky, North Star still smoldering.
Apples peeled and simmering tang the air,
and thoughts of warm cider make my mouth water.
It's hard to be sad in the clean sweep of clouds,
evergreens teasing this softer light. A wren lifts his throat
in song, notes you would have mimicked to give him answer,
the two of you in tête-à-tête until he flew away —
melody suspended, echoing in unexpected silence.

Time's Brief Shade

Confused, the roses sing summer,
afternoon crusted with clouds and chill.
We smuggle breath to you in kisses,
try not to hear your lungs crackle
as you rest your arms on the walker.

We are leaving and watch you scuffle
outside for the first time in nine days.
Your gaze around the neighborhood, the sky,
we sense the next world stenciled
under your skin, in your eyes.

Car backing out of the drive, we roll down the windows
to wave. You wave back,
wind gusting thin strands of your hair —
red blossoms dancing behind you.

How Light Leaves

Roses sigh their last promise —
late November and red petals
still star these graying days.

    Cardinals and woodpeckers edge out bluebirds
    and hummers at the feeder,
    crows lurking in bruised branches, arguing
    with squirrels, each other.

Leaves clutter the sidewalk,
the doorways, and it's time to pluck
tendrils of cobwebs from ferns
as I tug them inside before winter's bite.

    Earthquakes in Iraq, hurricanes in Ireland,
    mother nature blasts us,
    mocks our hubris.

Mars and Jupiter curve the sky —
twin planets of light, echoes
of Rome's rise and fall, autumn withering
and nights swelling dark, darker.

Pointillism: Morning

Clouds crescendo, and lightning,
stalked by thunder, fractures the sky.
Daffodils duck their heads like mooncalves,
lines of rain veining the yards and pebbling
the lemongrass, the lavender,
citrus and balsam suffusing the air.
Primroses pink the path from house to road —
a ghostly hope as day languishes,
hidden in fog and mist.

Before You're No Longer Here to Kiss

Cancer hovers, waning in a sky
bright with stars like dice —
June's velvet designs unlike winter's
close-wheeling constellations.
Streetlights glare, the rest of the world dark, asleep.
Out there, somewhere, bees quiver in their honeycombs,
fish skim mayflies and moss.
Mistletoe puckers on apple trees, oaks' rough branches —
ready to gather. But in sterile halls
hope shrivels.

The 24-hour deli clerk knows my order
by heart, just nods when I slip in
and stack scattered newspapers from the corner booth,
drop onto the slick vinyl.
Forehead on the window glass, my thoughts collide
with its chill, the pulsing fluorescence
and humming ovens.

The room reeks of onion and grease
unlike the bleach in the labyrinth where you lie.
One small space separate from others,
visiting hours suspended. When drips
and lasers and pills won't work,
what's wrong with dandelion seeds, shooting stars,
a cake crowded with wishing candles?
Summer may not be the right time,
but I'm grabbing all the mistletoe I can.

Night Fishers

Sky, fever-bright, urges dusk,
the moon. Boys mutter,
dip their lines, pucker the lake.
Empty of stars, darkness unfolds
until shadows converge,
a whippoorwill crooning matins.
Dried hydrangeas sculpt porch edges,
each rusted petal a tribute to holding on.
Unseen, a barred owl rustles the poplars,
skims a rabbit den, a shriek staining the air.
Empty-handed, the boys trudge home
in errant moonlight. Listen
as silence collapses around them.

Until the Raven Comes

The eye of the hummingbird delights
in bright, bold color — petals and stamens
of fuchsia, long throat of honeysuckle
to sneak, to tongue — beak parted,
devouring the solstice song of summer.

Sun and moon share this day,
gather the luster of the hummingbird's
wings, green shimmer pulsing the sky.

Wrens fold their melody into the wind.
Squirrels chuckle in the chestnut oak,
dashing above kayaks drifting
on the river's swell. Downstream, dusk
crouches on the horizon.

The Edge of Things

Summer breath stirs,
curves foxglove on the cliff side.

A grudge of rocks holds fast,
anchors grass and guano for nests,

screeches scouring the sky.
Rain drifts across the sea,

veils the breakers, the riprap —
tide sliding the sand from under my feet.

The Question of Rain

Frogs mumble in the weeds,
fireflies crowding the dark.
Chestnut oak leans, leaves browned
like scorched fruit, wounded
in persistent winter drought.
Hickories and pines burst skyward,
disappearing into dusk,
a haven for the grackles, the raccoons
as they shy from porch lights.
Thunderstorms tracking from the west,
we settle in for the coming storm.

Rhapsody of Ash

Gusts froth branches, drizzle beading
my face. Your voice in my head,
you are always here. A lifetime together accepts
no simple escape, and each room, each atom
I breathe reminds me of you. Where do I go from here?
Even the rain falls like tears before leaving.
The wind strokes, tangles my hair.
Your touch on my flesh will disappear,
your laughter will fade.
When silence descends, when no caress shivers my skin,
where will you be?

A gale force shudders harder now, blusters
like a nor'easter at its height, and I wonder
who whispers the hollow of your neck,
the arch of your foot? Who breathes warmth
across your chest, tongues your ear?
If the rain ever stops, if the wind ever quiets,
you still have my heart. You still have me.

Light Has No Mercy

—for Donald

When the phone rings in hushed stillness
of pre-dawn, before the larks stretch
their songs to the blue, to the blue —
it's not good news.

You didn't wake this last week —
eyes closed to fluorescent brightness,
to the pink cheer of painted daisies,
window shades blocked against copper sunsets.
Where were you,
                    wrapped in sleep-yet-not-sleep?

Rain and more rain
while I worked, bought milk and bread
before the storm, caught a cold,
cooked dinner — you channeled
your strength to cross that last bridge,
not looking back even as it crumbled behind you.

Fall Comes Weeping

Last year drought   this year rain
            already my friends are counting   their dead
        Lichen-scabbed trees host   commas of crows
    and we no longer know how to   breathe
        Under branches bare   trails worn
            until stone looks like bone
we watch rain smir   then plummet
        We stumble   into rooms gray
                    with light   bruising the corners
and our eyes reflecting   the darkness

The Weight of Snow

I know the days grow only shorter, blood
thickening with cold. Birch bark flakes,
trunks braced for wind and ice.
The creek whispers its way through the woods,
coaxing tongues of clay.
A cardinal skims branches under the meager sun —
fingers of white-gold barely stroking
the leaf-littered ground.
Thyme thrives slowly, my soul's silence deepening
with fog, with frost, and, finally,
with snow.

Winter's Edge

Trees refuse the surprise of snow,
commas of crows hunched
against December's wind.
Branches broken
                        against gray clouds.

      The muse, too, refuses mercy,
plucks random thoughts to slide like sleet
into my lines.   Rhythm and rhyme
trip, slip on the washer's buzzing,
the phone ringing, the neighbor's dogs.

Like a sprawling
                        faultline
the poem yawns   with   white   space
criss-crossed by arrows, splotches.
Words scratched out like crows
inked onto the winter sky.

Absence of Anything

Voices become echoes
in this mist swaddling the evening.
Horizon disguised: Forest or ocean? Root or edge?
Threads of fog curl closer,
even my hand blurs then vanishes.
The world narrows — mutes into resonance:
a towhee singing *Drink your te-e-ea!*
somewhere to the left,
distant waves rushing the shoreline.
Traffic, complaints, ringtones
clutter my brain,
but this vapor seeps into my skin,
cool breath shedding
the residue of my day. I am left
in a thickening silence
that lingers, enfolds, erases …

Brimming Dark

Lightning sizzles the verge, horizon smeared with rain.
Hot gusts of wind reach us before the storm,
and we struggle to reach the barn
before the sky bursts, fractures,
water and hail slapping the aged planks.

Trapped in gloom, we watch clouds
smother what's left of the light.
Thunder shocks, surprises us,
and we trudge farther into the darkness.
Ancient hay and horse scent the timbers —
the persistence of memory —
while rain staccatos, echoes the emptiness.

I stroke your arm, your back,
try to bridge the anger from this morning.
Water swamps the footpath,
and we are stuck in this place.
Gusts hiss around the wood, the tin,
something festering within.

Autumn Softness

Fog and shadow fall fast, last longer,
wren shivering in the hawthorn.
Dipped with gray, clouds perch
on the horizon, a crow coaxing his brothers
from hickory branches.
Mourning doves waggle around the yard
where I flung bread crumbs last night.
Mist whispers my cheek, my hair
curling in the damp.

Past the equinox and headed straight
for the solstice, each day surrenders
sooner to twilight.
I savor these hints of winter before it arrives —
sky dark, earth brushed with haze,
all of us breathing the in-between.

III. DARKER

Between us, the moon

aches, belly full as dawn
frays the edge of night.
In the shallows, a blue heron peers
into the lake, patient as Saint Francis.
But a quick slash of beak, and nature
reveals her unconcern.
Barely awake, the town unshutters,
signs turn in shop windows, blinds open.

And here we lie, in this bed so wide
we don't have to touch. I can't remember
the last time I knew you,
when you let me look in your eyes,
lean on you. What happened to us?
The heron unfolds its wings and lifts,
casts a shadow over the shore.
The moon pales, day empty and raw.

The Uncertain Hour

Dawn dusts the horizon pink,
night abandoned, stars swallowed
into the yawning blue.
Finches spiral the feeder,
grass patched in thistle,
wrens sifting the air with song.
Gone, midnight's musings —
your space empty, cold.
Only twisted sheets
to prove you were there at all.

Speak as if your lips could do anything

1.

Let the canyon curl around me,
      river be my guide
            What flows into you
flows out
      (after passing through)

Let the summer drought expose
      the foundation,
watch the mask crack,
         banks widen

      Let the flood fill me,
stretch my boundaries,
            my limits
      until it sweeps away inhibition

Let the snow pile high
         till it disguises every rock,
     every tree top
           and my vision
     is clear in dawn's bright silence

2.

It's always *they* who perpetrate,
we who are victims.
It is not him, not her.
It is you,
it is me.

Bullies in school locker rooms   mobs in Memphis parking
lots   terrorists at the Trade Center children sold for sex   women
silenced with fists and shame   men castrated in the fervor of
anti-work   The movies, the marathons, even the churches aren't
safe anymore   Don't let your hate define me

Death squads in Brazil, nuns raped in El Salvador, invasion in
Ukraine, executions in North Korea, and the earth keeps twisting
on its axis

Murder isn't a first world problem.
It's a head problem, a heart problem.
        It's a you and me problem.

3.

Icy and clear the creek rushes
                around my ankles and feet
        A junco flaps past
    then rests
            on a scarred and pitted stone
    Seed in beak, she hops close
            and I try not to move, to breathe
She's watching (me)

Jeffery pines climb the sky,
        one bruised and splintered
                    by lightning, and I wonder,
    as spring turns to summer
        where it will end
                    Where will we

Time is a Crooked Thing

We have to break the mirror to be ourselves. —May Sarton

Though *silver and exact*, the mirror has no memory.
No stop or start or rewind. Each day an exercise
in remembering who I am. Unremarkable, ordinary,
day unravels into day — brief bliss or grief to cling, to sift through,
to find myself again. Lines deepen, shadows darken,
and we must lean closer, ever closer to see.
Photos flaunt the proof. Had I shattered that mirror
when it first exposed the truth,
I could have hoarded the image of youth, the one my brain
still imagines, though my body begins its betrayal.
Squatting for the dropped sock, stooping to tie the shoe,
the petty aches and pains when cold weather comes,
when dawn silvers the sky with dew — oh, oh, I should have known
when the wren stopped singing the day was done.

How Cruel the Days

1.

Mind on getting to my second job,
I ate dinner in the car, listened
to the highway hum. Late afternoon sun
spied a brown mutt rambling
the road. A gap between cars,
in slow-motion I witnessed
the truck that did not stop,
saw her go down
and tires bounce across her twitching body —

2.

At eleven, I wanted to watch the men climb
our trees, see branches wobble then fall.
But I forgot to shut the door. Cooped inside
all morning, Duke wagged past, tail up,
nose to ground and zig-zagged the yard.
The snarling motor paused,
a limb dropped and rolled off —
my mother's face in the kitchen window,
sawdust drifting, settling in the sudden silence …

Darkness, Roaming

The moon withdraws.
Snow and ice spit the night,
a *ting, ting* on street signs,
windshields as we stride by,
breaths frosting the air.

Forewarned of the storm, days passed.
No hint in sight, we went back
to living. Cocooned
in the theater's snug womb,
another planet,
other lives mesmerized us.

Now, caught downtown in the flash
of traffic lights, we hurry to the car.
Wind bitters the branches, our skin.
A man shrouded in layers of scraps
sags into a doorway, and I turn my head.
What do we do with truth?

Clouds collapse the horizon,
buildings and treetops sheathed in white.
City muffled in numb flurries —
my vision obscured waiting for manna,
a pillar of fire in the ever-deepening snow.

Less Blossom, More Thorn

Snowflakes fur, cling to branches,
daffodils sagging, forsythia dusted white.
Early blue nurtured our hopes,
led us to believe in Spring.

The cost to redbuds, saucer magnolias
is loss of blush and bloom.
Acorns still shell the yard, withered oak leaves
another souvenir of the truth.

The moon shivers,
wild roses shuddering in the storm.

Edge of Emptiness

1.

The gorge gapes, hillside crowded
with broken bark, sizzling leaves —
summer's drought far away
but mountains burn, sear the blue.

Hemlocks bristle a seam of ridge
and sky, gray coiled in the clouds, the horizon —
what we can see of it. Crisp air pricks
the tips of our fingers, our feet.

2.

January, and we drowse before this fire,
cedar and pine spicing the rooms.
We wait for wisteria, daffodils,
anything like hope these overlong nights.

Anything to conjure the warbler's song
while we linger in darkness, moon rising.
You coming home
in your own pine box,
fire extinguished over the ocean.

World Drifting Darkly

Moonrise. Witch alders flash palely,
thrust of wind whispering the leaves.
A vireo warbles, charms purpling woods
then hushes as katydids chirr and squeal
    (loud, louder).
Crape myrtles rib the yard, currents of shadow
masking moths in their arches.

Pinched into paths, into boxes all day,
     my thoughts unwind.
Let the evening chorus   shift my senses,
my shoulders until the liquid air quenches
the clatter in my head. Until only Venus
                      disturbs the night.

Downstream, Light

No wind, but an arrow of geese
slices the sky, winter's brittle breath
still sculpting field and forest.
But the geese are back, coarse cries echoing
through the valley. Cattails thorn lake's edge,
silhouette of branches etched along the shore.
Shock of wings, of bodies settling
on water startles the deer, our hearts,
and we look up — watch the sun
blinding, blurring the horizon,
geese skimming the wrinkled surface
webbed feet furious and unseen.

Spring, Slouching

May-apple moon hazes a blue-gray dawn,
shivers in the watery sky. Rain all night.
House wrapped in mist, last autumn's leaves
surrender, wash away.

Mourning cloaks wing brown-velvet.
Irises spike the roadside, daffodils already dimming
as days lengthen, world rushing into spring —

not waiting for the clouds to clear,
not daring to wait as headlines of Vegas,
Sutherland Springs, Lakeland blast our dreams,
mire our nightmares.
        Stars gasping as they sink and drown.

Leaves, Sighing

This clay, heavy with my body, yields,
    fretwork of sycamores arcing overhead.
Limbs twist, divide the light, the rain
    as it slants through, tickles my face,
and I continue up the lane, hooded crows
    watching. What I would give
to share this day with you — sky half blue,
    half gray, droplets whispering to the leaves,
stroking the bark until it kisses the ground.

The Hardest Lesson

If the day was not your friend, she was your teacher. —Kimberly Nyogi

A dove growls in the hedgerow,
confessing from the woods,
a lament that bitters the evening.

> Doctors map your last days —
> a scaffold of words
> they assemble every day.

Late spring. The sun refuses
shrinking shadows
that rob blossoms' breath.

> The overheated room stifles me,
> but you sigh, shiver.

Swallows thorn the sky then swerve
toward the oaks in a chorus
as pines climb the purpling night.

Searching Between Branches

Fog clouds the valley,
not quite blue or white
here at the edge of dawn.
Sleepless night. Brain fuddled,
I watch the bluff stroked into color.
Haze dances under hues of pink and yellow,
harnesses my thoughts, pulse slowing.
The river horseshoes, almost circles
the village, creeks veining the outlying woods.
A breath of wind pushes through pines,
leaves already missing from oak and poplar
under days of steel and needling rain.
Like you, lost. Another day.

Adjusting the Light

Lightning wounds the sky,
scatters atoms of rain and vapor —
shifts the mask of shadows
squirming the edges of daybreak.

Hindered by clouds, the sun sulks —
noon a cool, silver-blue laced
with webs of mist, puddles of mud.

Wrens nestle in the boxwood,
nuthatch spiraling the oak
while I wash dishes, dream of spring,
stars blurring in the shutters of night.

Storing the Dark

A fist of starlight fractures clouds
          fastened on the horizon,
     sheets forgotten on the line
               when I pursued the ambulance from the house.
     Hydrangeas fuss and whisper,
doves grieving in their gloom,
               crust of moon in a leftover sky.

Mom's visit now a six-month sojourn,
          the garden grass, bent and worn,
               reveals the trail she paces every morning.
     Gait and gaze wandering, she strokes the chicory, the clematis.
               Mama, just for a moment we're happy.

               Windows still dark, I bundle the clothes,
          begin to smooth and fold.
Like her mother used to do in the gray dawn,
before day shifted into color, into tune.
Sprigs of lavender tucked into creases,
she bridged time and sorrow
with piles traded for stacks small enough
to set on a shelf, close the door, and walk away.

Shrine

An offering of seed, of worms and suet,
morning incomplete until I witness
bluebirds shaking feathers in the water,
wrens and chickadees plucking one kernel at a time
then gliding into low oak branches,
cardinals and thrushes on the feeder's pew.
The applause of starling wings.
A porch eave nest, smaller than my hand —
sanctuary for their chirping and chukking
long after the equinox translates dawn into melody,
an anthem better than stained glass.
I press my palm to the cool pane that separates me
from the flittering and jostling, the chirruping
that rises like incense. In the evergreens
a choir of crows waits to give the benediction.

IV. MORE LIGHT

Road, Beckoning

Moonrise and the raven road call.
Mist cowls the mountains,
copper leaves and duff scoured gray.
The promise of you hums
in the shadow,
                in the light.

A barred owl balances an oak branch,
head swiveling, crickets chirring
the wood line. Bitten by darkness,
moonlight wanders the trail, tempts me on —
tracing an echo
                of what used to be.

Afterimage

Pelican pierces the frothing surf,
      mackerel struggling against the pull of beak
          then gravity. Neck, wings arched,
     it climbs above the breakers
with bruising dawn. Scattering
        ashes of last night's fire,
    I discover embers still gleaming,
still seething. Sand crabs scuttle in the swash.
        Hard-packed silt, seaweed, shells somersault
    in the push and suck,
red-capped plovers silhouetted and rising.

Abundance of Shadow

Gray smudges the wide sky,
squirrels tucking acorns under roots,
in knot holes as day softens in the dwindling light.
Dried hydrangeas rib the sidewalk, cosmos fading,
petals falling one at a time.
Hummingbirds long gone, bees lumber
under the mums, legs brushed
with the last splurge of summer.

To be like the mole in curious darkness —
a gift to close my eyes in winter's den,
to quiet my heart, my thoughts,
to dream the Evening Star into spring's sunrise —
colors exploding, dissolving
the static that shrouds these days.

Seduction of Silence

Bees humming a mellow tune crisscross
the yard, percolate nectar
from hydrangeas and roses.
Wedged against the breadth of blue
butterflies binge on zinnias.
The eclipse in retrograde leaves a smoky taste,
the twilit haze suspended in a second's
quintessential stillness.
Wrens vanish in the juniper and crickets sough
the clover, doves mourning each shadow
as it disappears.

Leaving Town on the 8:05

A fringe of buildings, the last section
of town, then the rubbish, the rot
and, finally, into the open fields.
Framed by the clattering window, trees fist
the sky, and my sighs mist the view. What
to do now with the pulsing sway but shut
my eyes and wake to find the carriage dimmed.
Night throbs beyond the glass — lights spangling
the blackness. Day and time erased,
you slide into my mind, no holding you
back once you're in: remembering you
in the wrinkled sand, your hands tasting
the salt of my hips, surf singing
louder than these tracks beneath my breathing.

Summer Pours Out

—after AE Stallings

This morning's red and orange, a stained-glass wound
across the sky, awakens the pavement, the bus stop with blossoms
of color, butterflies lured from sleep. Patched shadows flicker, soar
into nothingness. Even the canopy of trees, that wilderness
of green, brightens in summer sun. Crows shout,
something harsh like a hurricane, a prairie fire growling.
Spiders coil their silk then stroke filaments that branch
into corners unseen, between brambles. But beetles rooting
at rose-hearts are disturbed by the hummingbirds' buzz and chuckle
as they dart and dip. The grass whispers
its secrets, shows thyme in the garden
how to spear then sprout. Though wasps and snakes burrow
in darkness, so, too, does the seed
that splits its own skin to grow and heal.

Breathing the Dark

Last night I was a child again   gripped by fear
    of a wolf   on my chest, eyes gleaming
into mine as I woke   in the dream.   Headlights
through my window,   twin beams that flared   my room,
    urged me to   struggle from my sheets,   stumble
the hall,   dim and small,   into their room.
    Warm darkness,   their breathing   a comfort.   I
tripped my way   to the bed, climbed in and slid   between
them.
    Whatever waited,   whatever
                followed,   here   I was safe.

Aching from the Light

We taste the rain as it slips
across the field. Like honey,
it soothes the rough tongue
of last year's drought:
yews patched brown, bare-limbed oaks
even through spring.

The grass, the very dirt hungered
for this day. We have waited
like crows for hymns of frogs,
for corn's milky ripeness,
our bellies to fill.

Wind picks up, shifts north,
and the rain whispers our shoulders.
Reminds us who we are.

These Trails

Forest fused with deadfall, moss girdles what's left
of oak and pine. Rhododendrons mingle with shadow,
sun breathing low and pale.
We walk these trails each week, watch the unfolding —
tips of green that presage warmer days.
A blue jay pursues us, bitters the woods with his cry.
Frost spurns teasing Spring, festers between gaps, laces slow eddies
before drifting into the falls, spiraling into mist and starspray.
Cold tickles our scarves, our cheeks, and we laugh
under branches stark but strong. You tug my sleeve, and we lean
into the wind, knowing this road will lead us home.

Out of its silver swell, the moon

slides into a spangled sky.
Midnight kisses the tip of my nose,
strokes my cheek as I sleep.
Flurries skip across fields, my dreams
and settle onto eaves, nestle into hickory branches
until a scattering becomes an ocean of white.
       Your fingers reach, graze ...
In winter's heart silence gathers
with the thickening snow,
our heat melting, steaming the night,
shafts of light sifting through the blinds
until I wake — secure against the frozen world,
snowdrift and starlight ascending.

Remember the Stars —

how you ached when you left
the lavish cloak of space,
became stardust then dew,
leaves and blossoms bright
with the last echoes of your light:

sparking, dancing,
licked by rain and by rivers
through riffles and pools
Magnolias blushing, mimosas feathering
between sky and earth, the groan
of loss rasps past —

a tune half-remembered in the wind,
on the wing of a wren,
a note lingering in the glitter path —
calling, drawing you home

Blossoms, Laced with Snow

Marooned in shadows of frost,
dogwoods blush with bloom.
The bluebird's throat unrusts,
song spinning across the dawn,
pouring through forsythia branches
tipped with gold.

Tufts of daffodils spark the yard.
Like a whirling compass needle,
Spring's gifts, chased by snow clouds,
blend into sullen shadows.
Crocus and violet taste the brittle air,
hide their buds in crumpled leaf scatter.

Soon this white weight, winter's last song,
will sigh under the sun, days lengthening,
hopeful and warm.

Green, Springing

Clouds sing hymns to the hills,
furrows etched like backstitches
embroidering the ground.
Across the lake, the refrain echoes,
and waterfalls patter a teasing language.
Ducks dabble through star grass
and floating heart, ducklings close by.

Breezes kiss the tips of trees —
pines whispering, maples murmuring
contralto tones. Honeysuckle brushes
invisible tendrils that wrap the bark,
lift limbs to greet
the moon blossoming overhead,
pale and fragile in the bluing day,
ripples of stars riding out the night.

First Light, Fading Dark

April coolness fiddles greening branches,
    cherry trees like pink smoke sweeping
across the mountain. Under a fading moon
    (large marble of a moon in a sky bruised
with clouds) wren and mockingbird root worms.

Unspoiled, this day offers its voice
    of mockingbird and towhee,
spider webs flawless, polished with dew —
    reversal of the late-night news
with its sordid lipstick, pancake makeup
    striving to disguise faces raw with triumph
over lives exploding, decisions twisted into nightmare.

Like slivers of glass, dawn fractures,
    crimson and gold fissuring the twilight —
reminder of an older rhythm, a pulse that tugs us
    back, thrusts us forward like the ocean tides,
like the moon giving way
    as the sun ignites wolf-gray skies.

Edge of Morning

Fog shawls, erases the horizon,
and I am invisible,
wrapped in a cocoon dense and endless.
From the porch even the roses lose
their pink, and the birds —
they are silent.
Except the crows.

Somewhere
beyond these muted clouds
and drifts of white
their *ah ah ah*s come muffled and hoarse.
Fig-colored shadows blur,
penstemon and fountain grass brushing the yard.

A vein of light grazes the mist,
fissures and fractures the vapor
as dawn sloughs thick cotton-wool,
daylight breaking clear and strong.

A Place to Breathe

The shape of your laughter is a temple. —Paul Bond

Laughter lingers on my doorstep —
morning daffodil-bright, apple blossoms drift
across the greening yard
where bluebirds ruffle in the feeder.
Last night rain thrashed, battered deep,
scoured the darkness and left it shiny with dew.

All right.
So the world still explodes,
cracks with anger and worry.
Hate tarnishes our tongues,
shoves it onto the unseen driver
of the car cutting into yesterday's commute,
the waitress pouring too-cold coffee.
The air sighs with lilac and hyacinth, a fragrance not lost —
not lost — to our better selves.

Wrens soften the day with song,
and my dog rolls, rubs her back in the drying grass.
My three-year-old neighbor squeals
at a butterfly, her stretching shadow.
Her giggles shimmer like a tambourine —
her music temple, a call for peace.

My Hands, Cracked Cups

When words breathe,
tongue the bark of birch
and flit through leaves,
whispering —

When embers burn to earth,
candelabra of branches
etched in sand
shifting, sifting into nothingness —

When threads connecting the stars
unravel, fray into daybreak,
to summon promises stroking
blood from stone —

carols of clouds will span
thyme and cosmos —
my heart braced, waiting
in longing and praise

Re-Creation

If blue is dream / what then innocence? —Federico García Lorca

It is the laughter of your three-year-old
　　neighbor when you sail soapy bubbles,
her fingers reaching
　　for the drifting moons

It's the adoration in your dog's eyes
　　when you nuzzle close and stroke his ears
even when shoe leather scatters the hallway

Your son's trust
　　when you subtract the training wheels,
when you run behind him
　　as he cycles away

It's your mother, losing her words
　　and her way, letting you lead her back
to the white-walled room, tuck her into bed

Iridescent, transparent,
　　reflective — the world balanced
on a quivering wand, forming

　　　　　　with your breath

Message to the Reader

In the cool quiet of early dawn
before even twilight changes to milky gray,
open your eyes. Gaze a moment at the ceiling.
Breathe once, twice, then slide
out of the warm burrow of sheets.
Face the darkness.
Stretch arms overhead — muscles pulling, straining
for day's adventure.
Stand at the window and examine the shadows,
      what light can be found.

Notes

Page 32   Smir: Scottish for *light drizzle*

Page 45   Line taken from Sylvia Plath's "The Mirror"

Page 57   Line taken from Thornton Wilder's *Our Town*

Page 66   A reverse-word sonnet: the first and last lines end in
            contrasting words, the second and thirteenth lines end
            in contrasting words, and so on to the center of the
            poem

About the Author

KB Ballentine received her MFA in Poetry from Lesley University, Cambridge, MA. She has participated in writing academies in the United States and Europe and holds graduate and undergraduate degrees in English.

She currently teaches high school theatre and creative writing and adjuncts for a local college. She also conducts writing workshops throughout the United States.

Published in numerous literary journals and anthologies, KB was a finalist for the 2006 Joy Harjo Poetry Award and a 2007 finalist for the Ruth Stone Prize in Poetry. KB received the Dorothy Sargent Rosenberg Memorial Fund Award in 2006 and 2007. KB was an Opera Omaha finalist in 2008, 2014 finalist for the Ron Rash Poetry Award, and received the Libba Moore Gray Poetry Prize in 2016.

Learn more about KB Ballentine at www.kbballentine.com.